Author's Note

W. Monson was born on October 18, 1925. She has been writing Christian poetry since her encounter with God and her realization of the gift of salvation by the death of God's Son, Jesus Christ.

W. Monson has numerous testimonies of which she has spoken. One is as follows:

"I continued to grieve over the loss of my son. He passed away at a very young age. He was 24 years old and took his own life. This was a very sad experience for all his family and friends. He had touched many of our lives. Months later, I still found it impossible to accept his death. My heart felt as though it was physically breaking. Day after day, I would kneel and pray for long periods of time. Early one morning, I was alone at home, kneeling and crying."

'Oh, Lord God in heaven,' I prayed. 'I just can not understand why my son had to die. He was so young. I loved him so very much. Why, God? Why did You take my son? I did not want to give him up.

"Suddenly, falling under conviction, I thought to myself, 'Who am I...to question God?'"

"It was then, I felt a warm hand on my shoulder. I heard a voice speak, 'I gave mine.'"

"I turned around to look. There was no one there."

TO MAN FROM GOD, Vol. 1

Holy Spirit Inspired

Prayers, Poems, Lyrics, and Raps

by

W. Monson and M. Monson,
Mother and Daughter

VISION PUBLISHING

Scripture taken from the New King James Version.
Copyright © 1982 by Thomas Nelson, Inc. Used by permission.
All rights reserved.

To Man from God, Vol. 1
Holy Spirit Inspired Prayers, Poems, Lyrics, and Raps

ISBN 978-0-9835799-0-8

Copyright © 2011 by W. Monson and M. Monson
First Edition

Vision Publishing
North Dakota
U.S.A.

Dedications by Permission

Printed in the United States of America. All rights reserved. No parts of this book may be reproduced or copied in any format or by any method unless prior written permission is obtained from the authors.

We would like to thank
the following people
for all their help
in making this book complete:

Lowell Monson
Louis Renfro, Sr.
Marlowe Monson
Corey Erwin
Thomas Monson
Zelma Renfro,
Lewis Renfro, Jr.
Sausha Renfro
Jacob Renfro

A special thank you to the artist, Gloria Van Dyke,
for teaching the author and illustrator that art
is not made to glorify man,
rather,
art is made
to reveal God's glory
through man.

All Original Artwork

Illustrations by
M. Monson and Z. Renfro

INTRODUCTION

The Living Waters
by Corey Erwin

Oh, dam not the living waters
On which sails my soul.
God, my Father, my creator,
Let them shimmer, let them flow.

Let the waters keep on rolling,
On through all my days,
Ever constant, always moving,
Streaming glory of His praise.

Let the waters keep on rolling,
On through every heart,
While along the way to Him,
God creates a work of art.

CONTENTS

Understand the Purpose	1
Get Ready, Church	3
All Praise to God	9
You Sent Your Spirit to Me	11
Truthful Gems	13
Every Day is Special Now	15
The Call of the Apostle Rap	17
Truthful Gems	19
Gladdening Joy	21
The Prisoners' Rap	23
Truthful Gems	25
All the Love	27
Healing Grace	29
Limitations	31
Fear Not, Little Flock	33
Truthful Gems	35

CONTENTS (Continued…)

A Prayer for My Family	37
Love	39
A Prayer for the Holy Spirit	41
Family of Love Marching Song	43
Message of the Prophet	45
I Need to be Like Jesus	47
Truthful Gems	49
The Witness	51
Truthful Gems	53
My Song of Praise	55
Beyond Compare	57
The Storm	59
Eternal Rest	61
Oh, Precious Name	63
I Thank Thee	65
From Heaven	67

CONTENTS (Continued…)

Truthful Gems	69
Peace Be Still	71
He is Our God	73
Free in Christ	75
Jesus is Everything to Me	77
Jesus, My Joy	79
Oh, Dear Lord of Mercy	81
Christ In Me	83
God Chose Me	85
Just Believe	87
Stumbling Up	89
Dear Lord, Save My Soul	91
A Prayer for My Mother	93
God's Gift of Love	95
To the Intellect	97
What is Born Again?	99

Understand the Purpose

All who look into this book
Will understand,
This is a book of love
From God to man.
For you,
Your brothers
And your sisters, too,
Are on The Vine,
That is,
The Son of God,
The Savior of mankind.

"Get Ready, Church" is dedicated to all churches truly governed by God the Father, God the Son, and God the Holy Spirit, specifically three faithfully include: First Lutheran Church, Litchville, North Dakota with Pastor Marcia Hegna; Glad Tidings Church, Casa Grande, Arizona with Pastor Roy Edwards and his wife, Greta; Cottonwood Church, Los Alamitos, California with Pastors Bayless and Janet Conley.

Matthew 16:18-19
18 And I also say to you that you are Peter, and on this rock I will build My church, and the gates of Hades shall not prevail against it. 19 And I will give you the keys of the kingdom of heaven, and whatever you bind on earth will be bound in heaven, and whatever you loose on earth will be loosed[d] in heaven."

Romans 11:29
29 For the gifts and the calling of God *are* irrevocable.

Revelation 2:7
7 "He who has an ear, let him hear what the Spirit says to the churches. To him who overcomes I will give to eat from the tree of life, which is in the midst of the Paradise of God.'"

GET READY, CHURCH

by M. Monson

Get Ready, Church -

You are the chosen ministry
Of Christ's missionary reconciliation,
Resting in the shadow
Of the Almighty Adoration.

As you have been tested, tried
And proven true
With spiritual stipulation,
By demonstrating God's love
For this lost and lamenting generation.

Get Ready, Church -
    Get Ready, Church -
        Get Ready, Church -
            For God has found you fit.

Obeying God's Word of love and truth,
You govern the hearts
That you commit.

Get Ready, Church -
For God is walking in your midst.

Get Ready, Church (Continued…)

Get Ready, Church -

You are the proverbial ambassadors
Of God's own, perfected prophesy,
Oracles foretold of sacrificial crucifixion
On Golgotha's tree.

By proclaiming Jesus Christ
As the Hidden Manna Mystery.
In overcoming death, Christ freed us,
And He leads us to eternity.

Get Ready, Church -
    Get Ready, Church -
        Get Ready, Church -
            For God has found you fit.

You are gifted and uplifted,
Attesting to
The curtain that He split.

Get Ready, Church -
For God is walking in your midst.

Get Ready, Church (Continued…)

Get Ready, Church -

You are pillars in God's Temple.
You are mustard seeds
Of fortified formations
With raised banners, promoting
The Prince of Peace
Throughout the nations.

You are irrevocably projected;
You are inevitably effective;
You are expressively protected and
Intentionally elected.

Get Ready, Church -
    Get Ready, Church -
        Get Ready, Church -
            For God has found you fit.

With love revealed, prayer appealed
Manifestations
Of the Holy Spirit.

Get Ready, Church -
For God is walking in your midst.

Get Ready, Church (Continued…)

Get Ready, Church -

The Savior has called you His friends,
And now you will receive
All the people He sends.
It is the Holy Spirit they hear groaning,
Pleading with the signs;

Unto you comes God's own
Remnant
Of lost children,
They are falling down in lines.
Through you God will be completing
His sealing
And the healing of their minds.

Get Ready, Church -
    Get Ready, Church -
        Get Ready, Church -
            For God has found you fit.

With glad tidings of praise,
The wise and knowing Word
You faithfully submit.

Get Ready, Church -
For God is walking in your midst.

Get Ready, Church (Continued…)

Get Ready, Church -

Paying tribute to the risen Son,
The Holy One,
The Great Shepherd of the Sheep,
Wearing God's love crown,
Sharing His profound
Principles you keep.

Souls of the Harvest awake within you,
Sought and brought
By the Lord to renew.
God's Right Hand swings open the view.
Tested and tried,
You have been proven true.

Get Ready, Church -
    Get Ready, Church -
        Get Ready, Church -
            For God has found you fit.

God's lampstands'
Galactic and
Glorious angels' fires are brightly lit.

You are His Church -
And God is walking in your midst.

"All Praise to God" is dedicated to the President of our great country, the United States of America.

Romans 13:1
¹ *Let every soul be subject to the governing authorities. For there is no authority except from God, and the authorities that exist are appointed by God.*

2 Corinthians 3:17
¹⁷ Now the Lord is the Spirit; and where the Spirit of the Lord *is*, there *is* liberty.

1 Peter 2:17
¹⁷ Honor all *people*. Love the brotherhood. Fear God. Honor the king.

ALL PRAISE TO GOD
by W. Monson

This world
Was lost in self and sin,
But Jesus came to seek,
The sinner, through
A shameful cross,
With love so pure and deep.

There was no other good enough
To all our sins forgive,
The Holy Son of God alone
Who died that we should live.

Before that blood stained cross
We kneel,
Upon His form to gaze,
Then humbly bow
Our contrite hearts,
And give Him all our praise.

Our Lord has lifted
Up from death,
The Savior, Lord, and King!
We worship Him of righteousness,
So death, where is your sting?

Our Father's Word to us is light.
We seek to know His will.
We ask not riches of this world,
But joy our hearts to fill.

Christ gives us wisdom
From above,
And courage,
By Your grace,
To reach out
To our fellow man,
And in him see Your face.

Bless this, our land.
Oh, hear us pray
To keep it safe and free.
Without Your guidance,
Lord,
We know
There is no liberty.

Now as we worship in
Your house,
Our eyes to You we raise.
We lift our voice in
Heart-felt thanks,
And
Give You all the praise.

"You Sent Your Spirit to Me" is dedicated to the First Lady of our great country, the United States of America.

Proverbs 31:10-12
10 Who[b] can find a virtuous[c] wife?
  For her worth *is* far above rubies.
11 The heart of her husband safely trusts her;
  So he will have no lack of gain.
12 She does him good and not evil
  All the days of her life.

Revelation 21:24
24 And the nations of those who are saved[l] shall walk in its light, and the kings of the earth bring their glory and honor into it.

YOU SENT YOUR SPIRIT TO ME
by M. Monson

There is a light I stand in,
It is my choice out of sin.
It is His Word that shows me the way.
If I stay in that light,
I can see wrong from right,
Not tomorrow, today is the day.
(1st Bridge) I was once a roaming nomad.
　　　　　　　I was just like tumbleweed.
　　　　　　　Then You sent Your Spirit to me.
　　　　　　　You fulfilled my every need.

(Refrain)
Hold me in Your presence, Lord.
Let me keep in constant prayer.
In Your sweet content,
I feel my heart relent,
As I seek Your service there.

YOU SENT YOUR SPIRIT TO ME (Continued...)

There is a lilt in my voice.
There is a skip in my step,
As I respond to the Spirit's plea.
Take me up to the throne.
You have made me Your own.
I believe. Here I am, Lord, use me.
(2nd Bridge) I was just an empty vessel.
                I was once a bitter soul.
                Then You sent Your Spirit to me.
                You have made my life joyful.
                (Repeat Refrain)

There is a road I walk on.
There is a rock I pray on.
There is a seed I sow with this song.
When the Word that I sing,
Is the Friend who will ring,
And will reign in the greatest love song.
(3rd Bridge) I was once a clanging cymbal.
                I was just a sounding gong.
                Then You sent Your Spirit to me,
                And Your love made me a song.
                (Repeat Refrain)

Truthful Gems

Psalm 34:7
7 The angel[a] of the LORD encamps all around those who fear Him,
And delivers them.

Psalm 91:11
11 For He shall give His angels charge over you,
To keep you in all your ways.

Matthew 24:31
31 And He will send His angels with a great sound of a trumpet, and they will gather together His elect from the four winds, from one end of heaven to the other.

Hebrews 13:2
2 Do not forget to entertain strangers, for by so *doing* some have unwittingly entertained angels.

"Every Day is Special Now" is dedicated to all Sunday School teachers who have given of their love and skill to children, so the children can tell others of God's message of love to the world with no one excluded.

Deuteronomy 26:18-19
[18] Also today the LORD has proclaimed you to be His special people, just as He promised you, that *you* should keep all His commandments, [19] and that He will set you high above all nations which He has made, in praise, in name, and in honor, and that you may be a holy people to the LORD your God, just as He has spoken."

EVERY DAY IS SPECIAL NOW
by W. Monson

Monday is a happy day,
I greet each week anew,
Since Jesus washed my sins away
And cleansed me through and through.

Tuesday morning I am glad,
As I find time to pray.
I kneel in honor to His name,
And bid Him guide my way.

Wednesday, I rejoice in love.
My Jesus is divine.
He reaches down
From up above,
To touch this
Heart of mine.

Thursday, how
I marvel at
His awesome
Love for me.
To think He died
Upon the cross,
His love has set me free.

Friday, He gives strength
To walk,
I pray to know His will.
I lift my eyes up heavenward.
He whispers,
"Peace. Be still."

Saturday, I labor hard
To touch some lonely hearts,
And spread about the joyous love
That Jesus Christ imparts.

Sunday, finds me in His church.
Oh, joy to worship there.
I join in loving fellowship,
With other hearts that care.

Every day is special now,
Lord Jesus I proclaim,
I sing about His love for me
And praise His Holy Name.

"The Call of the Apostle Rap" is dedicated to Pastor Tommy Barnett, Dream Center Founder and his son, Pastor Matthew Barnett, Dream Center Co-Founder and Pastor Matthew's wife, Pastor Caroline Barnett.

John 15:5-8
5 "I am the vine, you *are* the branches. He who abides in Me, and I in him, bears much fruit; for without Me you can do nothing. 6 If anyone does not abide in Me, he is cast out as a branch and is withered; and they gather them and throw *them* into the fire, and they are burned. 7 If you abide in Me, and My words abide in you, you will[b] ask what you desire, and it shall be done for you. 8 By this My Father is glorified, that you bear much fruit; so you will be My disciples.

Ephesians 2:19-22
19 Now, therefore, you are no longer strangers and foreigners, but fellow citizens with the saints and members of the household of God, 20 having been built on the foundation of the apostles and prophets, Jesus Christ Himself being the chief corner*stone,* 21 in whom the whole building, being fitted together, grows into a holy temple in the Lord, 22 in whom you also are being built together for a dwelling place of God in the Spirit.

THE CALL OF THE APOSTLE RAP
by M. Monson

Are you the lonely one and walkin' heart-stone cold?
Are you bound and blind on a wayward road?
Along the edge of a deep dark void,
Pushed out upon the ledge of paranoid.
Do the lights shine too bright,
And your feet turn code-blue?
And you can not stop what you should not do,
At Satan's store for a chill crime dime,
You cry the lie, "Just one more time!"

(Hook)
Can you hear the knock?
(Knock-knock! Knock-knock! Knock-knock!)
Can you hear the call?
(Apostle? Apostle? Apostle?)
This is God with His wisdom,
And you are called, and you must come.
The Lord of all has anointed you!
Abba, God has appointed you!
With an ear to hear, with an eye to see,
To give account of His prophesy.

(First Chorus)
It is the Lord with His sure covenantal proclamation.
He has favored you with heavenly elation.
Now you can ring the Spiritual revelation,
So you can sing with the Redeemer's rejuvenation,
Encircled in His love and predestined destination.

THE CALL OF THE APOSTLE RAP (Continued...)

Are you downward wound around on the serpent's tail?
Insecure with fear—thinking you will fail.
Your will is weak—seeing your hands shake,
Captivated by the old slingin' snake.
Does your blistered soul beg for one more, long-held breath?
Do you bend your head to indulge in your own death?
You sink inside the destroyer's choke.
You gave all you had for the smoke.
(Repeat Hook)

(Second Chorus)
It is God with His eternal, justifying safe embrace.
He instills prophetic fire to light your face,
Now you can run the great and gratifying race,
With His holy unifying and all abiding grace!
Christ is the true love vine,
That prunes your branch held into place.

Are you slipping in shame and sinking limping lame?
Are you paining aimless to gain the game?
The stake you pound only flags defeat,
Riddled and whittled by lawless deceit.
Are you slamming the door daring not to care?
Are you telling someone to pay your share?
Angry words you flare become goodbye.
The last one to leave will shake your cry.
(Repeat Hook)

(Third Chorus)
Because the Lord with His own merciful sanctification,
Has selected you from all of His creation,
Now you can join the charismatic celebration,
Now you can dance with evangelistic jubilation,
And lead one-by-one individual's soul salvation.

Truthful Gems

Isaiah 50:4
4 "The Lord GOD has given Me
The tongue of the learned,
That I should know how to speak
A word in season to *him who is* weary.
He awakens Me morning by morning,
He awakens My ear
To hear as the learned.

Luke 15:7
7 I say to you that likewise there will be more joy in heaven over one sinner who repents than over ninety-nine just persons who need no repentance.

John 4:24
24 God *is* Spirit, and those who worship Him must worship in spirit and truth."

1 Corinthians 12:28
28 And God has appointed these in the church: first apostles, second prophets, third teachers, after that miracles, then gifts of healings, helps, administrations, varieties of tongue.

"Gladdening Joy" is dedicated to Ernest and C. Rochelle Grubbs, Litchfield Park, Arizona, in whose lives the light of the living God shines within.

Psalm 80:3
3 Restore us, O God;
Cause Your face to shine,
And we shall be saved!

2 Corinthians 4:6
6 For God, who said, "Let light shine out of darkness,"[a] made his light shine in our hearts to give us the light of the knowledge of the glory of God in the face of Christ.

GLADDENING JOY
by W. Monson

Dear Jesus,
As at Your
Feet I kneel,
With awe and
Penitent praise
In prayer
As oft' I've come
Before,
To Thee
Adore,
And leave
My burdens
There.

With heart
So full of gladdening
Joy,
My sorrow all replaced
With love
By grace,
Because again
My heart is clean,
And I have seen
The Essence of
Your Face.

"The Prisoners' Rap" is dedicated to the Innocence Project, of which co-founders and Co-Directors, Attorneys Barry Scheck and Peter Neufeld are pursuing justice for prisoners wrongly convicted.

Psalm 116:13
13 I will take up the cup of salvation,
  And call upon the name of the LORD.

Isaiah 42:5-7
5 Thus says God the LORD,
  Who created the heavens and stretched them out,
  Who spread forth the earth and that which comes from it,
  Who gives breath to the people on it,
  And spirit to those who walk on it:
6 " I, the LORD, have called You in righteousness,
  And will hold Your hand;
  I will keep You and give You as a covenant to the people,
  As a light to the Gentiles,
7 To open blind eyes,
  To bring out prisoners from the prison,
  Those who sit in darkness from the prison house.

THE PRISONERS' RAP
by M. Monson

The buzz is out—that the Lord is in.
The Man of Peace has risen within.
The barred walls of prison—where the prisoners shout -
That the shout is out—that the shout with clout
Is the Buzz of Love…
Because…He…Was…
Born to be stabbed and born to be hung.
Born to sting the unjustified tongue.
Born to die for the downtrodden soul.
To insure with the promise and to provide with the proof.
To unlatch the harness and cut loose the noose,
So that the prisoners' necks are not in the show.
They are not in the dust of the crust—and buried below.
Down, down below.
In dark Sheol.

(Hook)   You are not neglected—forbidden or forgotten.
             You are not rejected—the Lord has begotten -
             Your vindication.
             We rap with elation
             That the Lord of creation,
             That the Lord of the nation
             Has chosen you—for exoneration.

(Chorus) He is the promised one—He is God's own son.
             And you were chosen, too, before life begun.
             He is our choice—He is our voice.
             He is our cue—to fight for you.
             Until the battle is done—until the race is won.
             Until the Son has come.

We are the salt.
It is the season.
This is the time.
And you are the reason.

THE PRISONERS' RAP (Continued...)

The track is out—that the truth is on.
The buzz came back—to defeat the wrong.
War weapons of smack—push spiritual hood,
To destroy the crash and preserve the good.
It is the track of love…
Because…He…Was…
Struck in the face—betrayed by a friend.
Flogged with the switch—and brave to the end.
You do not owe the sin of the grim,
And with mighty assurance you called upon Him.
To open the well—the well where you fell.
Not guilty! You still bore the blame.
You called Christ's name.
You will not stay in the cell where the criminals dwell.
You will rise on up.
Saved by the cup.

(Repeat Hook) (Repeat Chorus)

The words we rap—are from heaven's vent.
The word is out—that the Buzz is sent.
The crushing bars brake—for the unfair shake.
And the choke is broke—by a new love yoke.
It is the word of love…
Because…He…Was…
In the ground and alive in the grave.
Born to crave and save the prisoner slave.
They set you up in the day,
They tried to make you pay.
When Salvation's Helmet and the Spirit Sword heard they lied,
God fought on the innocent side.
You are not caught in the net they set.
It is the Lord you met when you called on the king.
Freedom has rung.
Freedom will ring.

(Repeat Hook) (Repeat Chorus)

Truthful Gems

Exodus 14:14
[14] The LORD will fight for you, and you shall hold your peace."

Zechariah 8:16
[16] These are the things you shall do: Speak each man the truth to his neighbor; Give judgment in your gates for truth, justice, and peace;

Joel 2:21
[21] Fear not, O land; Be glad and rejoice, For the LORD has done marvelous things!

2 Peter 3:9
[9] The Lord is not slack concerning *His* promise, as some count slackness, but is longsuffering toward us,[b] not willing that any should perish but that all should come to repentance.

1 John 2:25
[25] And this is the promise that He has promised us—eternal life.

"All the Love" is dedicated to Diane Silk, Lakewood, California, a woman of truth who loves Jesus.

Proverbs 27:9
⁹ Ointment and perfume delight the heart,
    And the sweetness of a man's friend *gives delight* by hearty counsel.

Philippians 1:9-10
⁹ And this I pray, that your love may abound still more and more in knowledge and all discernment, ¹⁰ that you may approve the things that are excellent, that you may be sincere and without offense till the day of Christ,

1 John 4:16
¹⁶ And we have known and believed the love that God has for us. God is love, and he who abides in love abides in God, and God in him.

ALL THE LOVE
by W. Monson and M. Monson

All the love I have for Jesus,
He has asked that I proclaim,
I will shout it from the rooftop,
He will call me by my name.

    (Refrain)
    Trusting, trusting, always trusting,
    In the presence of the Lord, I stand.
    Trusting, trusting, always trusting,
    The Lord Jesus holds my hand.

In the pages of the Bible,
I will hear each word He speaks,
I will do what He commands me,
I will be the friend He seeks.
(Repeat Refrain)

In His vineyard, I am growing,
As a branch abiding here,
God will keep me in His garden,
I will bloom while He is near.
(Repeat Refrain)

All the love I have for Jesus,
He has given me to share.
He will open heaven's gateway,
I will come to Him in prayer.
(Repeat Refrain)

"Healing Grace" is dedicated to Doctor Suresh V. Balenalli, Casa Grande, Arizona, a doctor who is enabled by God to care for and help others with the knowledge he has been blessed with.

Proverbs 2:6
6 For the LORD gives wisdom;
    From His mouth *come* knowledge and understanding;

Matthew 4:23
23 And Jesus went about all Galilee, teaching in their synagogues, preaching the gospel of the kingdom, and healing all kinds of sickness and all kinds of disease among the people.

HEALING GRACE
by W. Monson

Like comes the dawn,
    So comes God's Word
        Into the heart that never heard.
    The joy, expression of the peace,
For loving grace that will not cease.

My hearing ears
    That did not hear,
        Oh sin-blind eyes that would not see.
    Forgive my sin; cast out my fear,
Thou essence of eternity.

Heal my body
    And heal my spirit,
        By grace, I cannot claim to merit.
    Thy promise now I make my own,
For healing comes from Thee alone.

"Limitations" is dedicated to the Open Door Center in Valley City, North Dakota. Consideration is given to all the people associated with this care giving facility that demonstrates true concern for the clients they serve: Bill Cook, President of the Board of Directors; Mary Simonson, Executive Director; Cindy Weisenburger, Program Director; other staff and employees.

Job 11:7
7 "Can you search out the deep things of God? Can you find out the limits of the Almighty?

1 Corinthians 13:13
13 And now abide faith, hope, love, these three; but the greatest of these *is* love.

LIMITATIONS
by W. Monson

I cannot make the sun
To rise,
However strong I'd be.
I cannot fill the sky
With blue,
Nor still a rolling sea.

I cannot make
A rainbow,
Nor
Wash the
Trees
With rain.
I cannot
Make
A bird
To sing,
Nor ripen
Fields
Of grain.

I cannot
Make the
Sun to set,
Nor hang the amber
Moon.
I cannot usher in the
Dawn, nor warm the
Day at noon.

I cannot light a firefly,
Nor catch the early dew.
I cannot build a
Mountain high,
With peaks
Of purple
Hue.

I cannot
Measure
Up
To that
Which
God
Would
Have me
Be,
But I can
Shout about
His love,
He gave
His Son for me!

God's world
Is filled with
Many things
That I could never do.
But I can build
A bridge of love
To reach
From me to you.

"Fear Not, Little Flock" is dedicated to a woman with a heart of love, Lois Hofmann, the Coordinator of the DOVES, Fargo, North Dakota.

Psalm 23
A Psalm of David.

1 The LORD *is* my shepherd;
   I shall not want.
2 He makes me to lie down in green pastures;
   He leads me beside the still waters.
3 He restores my soul;
   He leads me in the paths of righteousness
   For His name's sake.
4 Yea, though I walk through the valley of the shadow of death,
   I will fear no evil;
   For You *are* with me;
   Your rod and Your staff, they comfort me.
5 You prepare a table before me in the presence of my enemies;
   You anoint my head with oil;
   My cup runs over.
6 Surely goodness and mercy shall follow me
   All the days of my life;
   And I will dwell[a] in the house of the LORD
   Forever.

Luke 12:32
32 "Do not fear, little flock, for it is your Father's good pleasure to give you the kingdom.

FEAR NOT, LITTLE FLOCK
by W. Monson

Fear not, little flock, our Shepherd is praying,
In the dark garden of Gethsemane.
Praying, "The Father, this cup pass away,"
Yet yielding His will for you and for me.

Refrain
Fear not, little flock, to the Shepherd draw near.
He goes before you; there's nothing to fear.

Fear not, little flock, our Shepherd is dying.
He hangs on the cross at cruel Calvary.
His death is not lasting; He will arise
On bright Easter morning. Watch. You will see.
(Repeat Refrain)

Fear not, little flock, our Shepherd has risen.
Come to the dark tomb and there look inside.
"He is not here," says the bright angel.
The stone is rolled back, the opening wide.
(Repeat Refrain)

Fear not, little flock, our Shepherd is knocking,
At the door of your hearts. Oh, let him in.
For He is longing, waiting to enter,
He comes to forgive and wash away sin.
(Repeat Refrain)

FEAR NOT, LITTLE FLOCK (Continued...)

Fear not, little flock, our Shepherd's ascending.
With the Dear Father, He now intercedes,
Pleading forgiveness for all who have strayed.
Giving us comfort and strength for our needs.
(Repeat Refrain)

Fear not, little flock, our Shepherd is sending
His Holy Spirit to guide all our ways.
To open God's Word for all His people.
To lead in His footsteps all of our days.
(Repeat Refrain)

Fear not, little flock, our Shepherd is leading
Us to green pastures where we will find rest.
With open arms, the Father is waiting.
Why linger outside? Come in and be blessed.
(Repeat Refrain)

Fear not, little flock, our Shepherd is seated,
Where flows at His feet, the river of peace.
Before the great throne, bow and adore Him.
Sin cannot enter and light will not cease.
(Repeat Refrain)

Truthful Gems

Psalm 55:17
¹⁷ Evening and morning and at noon
   I will pray, and cry aloud,
      And He shall hear my voice.

Jeremiah 23:4
⁴ I will set up shepherds over them who will feed them; and they shall fear no more, nor be dismayed, nor shall they be lacking," says the LORD.

Matthew 9:38
³⁸ Therefore pray the Lord of the harvest to send out laborers into His harvest."

Matthew 21:22
²² And whatever things you ask in prayer, believing, you will receive."

2 Timothy 1:7
⁷ For God has not given us a spirit of fear, but of power and of love and of a sound mind.

"A Prayer for My Family" is dedicated to the Blue Grass Association of North Dakota (B.A.N.D.) with John Andrus, Litchville, North Dakota. The many associates of B.A.N.D. express their gifts and talents from God with entertaining and inspirational music.

Psalm 28:7
7 The LORD *is* my strength and my shield;
    My heart trusted in Him, and I am helped;
    Therefore my heart greatly rejoices,
    And with my song I will praise Him.

A PRAYER FOR MY FAMILY
by M. Monson

I pray, Oh Lord, how long will the enemy be strong,
As the battle rages on and on around me?
Call us each by our new name,
May we never be the same,
Lord, take away the pain from my family.

(Refrain)
And I know my Christ is standing,
Standing and staying,
Patiently waiting,
Watching me praying.
And while I am praying,
I can hear my loved ones saying,
Saying Jesus died for us, just because He loves us.

Choose each one for Your own, Lord,
And for our sins atone.
Help us find Your final home as our destiny.
Always be our faithful guide,
Always stronger at our side,
Let Your arm by us abide,
More intently.
(Repeat Refrain)

In faith let us acclaim, Jesus took away the blame,
And let heaven be our aim for eternity.
Yes, the battle has been long,
But the enemy was wrong,
And our deaths are swallowed up in victory.
(Repeat Refrain)

"Love" is dedicated to Stephan Zajac, Casa Grande, Arizona, a man of great faith and love.

Luke 10:30-36

30 Then Jesus answered and said: "A certain *man* went down from Jerusalem to Jericho, and fell among thieves, who stripped him of his clothing, wounded *him,* and departed, leaving *him* half dead. 31 Now by chance a certain priest came down that road. And when he saw him, he passed by on the other side. 32 Likewise a Levite, when he arrived at the place, came and looked, and passed by on the other side. 33 But a certain Samaritan, as he journeyed, came where he was. And when he saw him, he had compassion. 34 So he went to *him* and bandaged his wounds, pouring on oil and wine; and he set him on his own animal, brought him to an inn, and took care of him. 35 On the next day, when he departed,[i] he took out two denarii, gave *them* to the innkeeper, and said to him, 'Take care of him; and whatever more you spend, when I come again, I will repay you.' 36 So which of these three do you think was neighbor to him who fell among the thieves?"

LOVE
by M. Monson

"You are mine," God said,
When He claimed me for His own.
This decision He made
Was upon His judgment throne.
What He ruled was just and right, I would agree.
Yet then, "Oh, my God?" I ask again,
"Why should You have chosen me?"

As a child of God, I must obey each command,
Listening carefully to His Word to understand,
Just what it is I must expect from myself,
"It is to love
Only Me as God,
And your neighbor as yourself."

I understand that loving my Lord God is right.
I love Him with my mind,
Heart and soul, and all my might.
"But, God, who is my neighbor
To love like me?"
His answer?
"It is anyone in need of charity."

"A Prayer for the Holy Spirit" is dedicated to John and Sharon Moss of Mesa, Arizona, who are filled with the Holy Spirit.

Psalm 51:10-11
¹⁰ Create in me a clean heart, O God,
    And renew a steadfast spirit within me.
¹¹ Do not cast me away from Your presence,
    And do not take Your Holy Spirit from me.

Matthew 3:11
¹¹ I indeed baptize you with water unto repentance, but He who is coming after me is mightier than I, whose sandals I am not worthy to carry. He will baptize you with the Holy Spirit and fire.[b]

A PRAYER FOR THE HOLY SPIRIT
by W. Monson

Heavenly Father,
Thy goodness transcends
All of men's thinking,
As it descends.
From evil deceit, our life it defends;
On Thy great forgiveness
Our spirit depends.

Keep us today
From selfish in-growing,
In response to forgiveness,
Our life all a-glowing,
Thy Holy Spirit our hearts overflowing,
That others may see Thy love in us showing.

The need of our brother
In day-to-day living,
We will allay through day-to-day giving.
Thus, sheep for Thy pasture,
We shall be achieving,
While loneliness, pain,
And heartache relieving.

"Family of Love Marching Song" is dedicated to LtCol Charles Erwin, Retired Assistant Director of the United States Marine Band, and his wife, Mary Lou. They have spent their lives serving the Lord.

Psalm 108:1-4
1 O God, my heart is steadfast;
   I will sing and give praise, even with my glory.
2 Awake, lute and harp!
   I will awaken the dawn.
3 I will praise You, O LORD, among the peoples,
   And I will sing praises to You among the nations.
4 For Your mercy *is* great above the heavens,
   And Your truth *reaches* to the clouds.

FAMILY OF LOVE MARCHING SONG
by M. Monson

God is the One-Two-Three,
The Holy Deity,
And He is certainly,
The one eternally,
The richest charity,
The worthy rarity.
He is assuredly,
The opportunity,
For immortality,
Through Christianity,
For all humanity.
Oh, my God! Oh, my God!

(Refrain)
The Father, the Spirit,
The Son,
Family of Love,
Three-In-One.
The Father, the Spirit,
The Son,
Great glory above!
Family of Love.
Oh, God!

God is the One-Two-Three,
The Holy Trinity.
He is impressively,
The one infinity,
The sure philosophy,
The true theology,
He is exclusively,
The opportunity,
For immortality,
Through Christianity,
For all humanity.
Oh, my God! Oh, my God!
(Repeat Refrain)

God is the One-Two-Three,
The Holy Trilogy.
He is enduringly,
The grand epitome,
The one reality,
Lasting totality.
He is with clarity,
The opportunity,
For immortality,
Through Christianity,
For all humanity.
Oh, my God! Oh, my God!
(Repeat Refrain)

God is the One-Two-Three,
The Holy Unity.
He is extensively,
The vastest rhapsody,
The only liberty,
The happy jubilee.
He is personally,
The opportunity,
For immortality,
Through Christianity,
For all humanity.
Oh, my God! Oh, my God!
(Repeat Refrain)

"Message of the Prophet" is dedicated to the churches with the Revival Ministries preaching through the Holy Spirit.

Numbers 12:6
⁶ Then He said, "Hear now My words: If there is a prophet among you, I, the LORD, make Myself known to him in a vision; I speak to him in a dream.

Revelation 22:1
¹ And he showed me a pure[a] river of water of life, clear as crystal, proceeding from the throne of God and of the Lamb.

Message of the Prophet
By M. Monson

It is the coming of the ages —
Hear the words the prophet said,
Within a great awakening from the rising of the dead,
Hidden from the locust's smoldering pit that was unearthed,
Rescued by God's heavenly lamb,
Each spirit is re-birthed.

It is the coming of the ages —
Faithful telling of God's Word,
Holy Spirit revelation will translate the tongues we heard,
Accompanied by a fire that burns above the brow,
A sign unto the nations that the Lord is coming now.

It is the coming of the ages —
Bleeding vision of the moon,
Falling, withered, broken branches
Cut by God's diffusing prune
Are grafted in again through faith from the Majestic Lord,
Anointed with the oil the Holy Spirit has outpoured.

It is the coming of the ages —
God's true path to life was chose.
Hence administering angels come to trumpet blowing woes,
From forth the River Church the Holy Spirit will not rest,
Facing madness, tempest, darkness,
The prophet stood the test.

It is the coming of the ages —
The good news has fast been sent.
The message that was spoken
Acclaims man's time on earth is spent.
Humbly kneeling at His kingdom appearing in the sky
Our heads will bow in union
When God's River rolls on high.

"I Need to be Like Jesus" is dedicated to the Full Gospel Interdenominational Churches led by the Spirit of the Lord.

John 14:12-13
12 "Most assuredly, I say to you, he who believes in Me, the works that I do he will do also; and greater *works* than these he will do, because I go to My Father. 13 And whatever you ask in My name, that I will do, that the Father may be glorified in the Son.

Matthew 13:34-35
34 All these things Jesus spoke to the multitude in parables; and without a parable He did not speak to them, 35 that it might be fulfilled which was spoken by the prophet, saying:
*" I will open My mouth in parables;
I will utter things kept secret from the foundation of the world."*

I NEED TO BE LIKE JESUS
by M. Monson

Let me rise
With the rising of the sun
Praising Jesus.
Let me speak through the daytime
With His name upon my lips.
Let the setting of the sun
Still hear me praising Jesus,
I want to worship in the Lord's Sanctuary.
    I want to be like Jesus.
    I want to pray as He taught.
    I need to tell the lame - walk!
    The deaf and mute to hear and talk!
    I have Spiritual Resurrection.
    I will join His Grand Ascension.
    I will seek out what He sought.

I NEED TO BE LIKE JESUS (Continued...)

Let me lead with the glory
Of the Lord shining on me.
Let me sing with the angels of the Lord
Right beside me.
Let me call out to the heavens
To our God up above me,
I want to worship in the Lord's Sanctuary.
    I want to be like Jesus.
    I want to say what He said.
    I need to cast out demons.
    I need to raise the worldly dead.
    I have His Spiritual Dimension.
    I will join His Grand Ascension.
    I will follow where He led.

Let me stand with my testimony all about Jesus.
Let me boldly and bravely
Inform the world He saved me.
Let the words that I say
Reach someone else today,
I want to worship in the Lord's Sanctuary.
    I want to be like Jesus.
    I need to heal the lepers.
    Be one of His disciples,
    Who preach His priceless parables.
    I have His Spiritual Redemption.
    I will join His Grand Ascension.
    I will work with miracles.

Truthful Gems

Isaiah 58:8
⁸ Then your light shall break forth like the morning, Your healing shall spring forth speedily, And your righteousness shall go before you; The glory of the LORD shall be your rear guard.

Psalm 30:2
² O LORD my God, I cried out to You,
  And You healed me.

Matthew 15:30
³⁰ Then great multitudes came to Him, having with them the lame, blind, mute, maimed, and many others; and they laid them down at Jesus' feet, and He healed them.

James 5:16
¹⁶ Confess *your* trespasses[a] to one another, and pray for one another, that you may be healed. The effective, fervent prayer of a righteous man avails much.

"The Witness" is dedicated to the Nondenominational churches organized in the United States that are rallying to encourage people to come to the Lord and be ready to change their lives with God's Spirit.

Isaiah 64:8
8 But now, O Lord, You are our Father; We are the clay, and You the potter; And all we are the work of Your hand.

Jeremiah 18:2
2 "Arise and go down to the potter's house, and there I will cause you to hear my words."

Acts 1:8
8 But you shall receive power when the Holy Spirit has come upon you; and you shall be witnesses to Me[a] in Jerusalem, and in all Judea and Samaria, and to the end of the earth."

THE WITNESS
by M. Monson

Let Your Word be a fountain
That flows, Lord,
Flows into the hearts of the lost.
May we witness unto the broken
That Dear Jesus has paid all the cost.
God will loosen the sin that is pressing,
Threatening to tear lives apart.
He will lift us out of death's doorway,
As the Lord Jesus enters their heart.

(1st Refrain)
And together we will ask Him,
And together we will pray.
God's healing waters of life,
Will wash the pain away.

Let our eyes be the eyes of the Shepherd,
Searching for His sheep that have strayed.
Take us into the seas of the world
Where the wounded
And wayward have stayed.
Let us reach for their hand
With the Scripture,
God will lift us up with His Word.
He will lead us out of the deep
As the name of our Jesus is heard.

THE WITNESS (Continued...)

(2nd Refrain)
Then together we will witness,
Then together we will tell,
God's saving all His lost sheep,
He pulls them from the swell.

Let our lips be love beacons of light, Lord,
Let them beckon all souls unto You.
May we lead from out of the darkness
Refreshing our spirits anew.
We will enter into the Potter's House,
Rejoicing and happy we came,
Removing all shackles of sorrow,
By exalting and praising God's name.

(3rd Refrain)
Then together we will worship,
Then together we will sing.
We're glowing from the service,
The service of our King.

Truthful Gems

Job 12:12
¹² Wisdom *is* with aged men,
   And with length of days, understanding.

Job 28:28
²⁸ And to man He said,
   'Behold, the fear of the Lord, that *is* wisdom,
   And to depart from evil *is* understanding.'"

Job 32:8
⁸ But *there is* a spirit in man,
   And the breath of the Almighty gives him understanding.

Psalm 14:2
² The LORD looks down from heaven upon the children of men,
      To see if there are any who understand, who seek God.

Proverbs 11:12
¹² He who is devoid of wisdom despises his neighbor,
    But a man of understanding holds his peace.

"My Song of Praise" is dedicated to the Women's Bible Study Group with Pastor Karen Locklear, Prayer Warrior Betty Tate and the many Prayer Warriors with the Glad Tidings Church, Casa Grande, Arizona.

1 Peter 5:4
[4] and when the Chief Shepherd appears, you will receive the crown of glory that does not fade away.

1 John 5:14-15
[14] Now this is the confidence that we have in Him, that if we ask anything according to His will, He hears us. [15] And if we know that He hears us, whatever we ask, we know that we have the petitions that we have asked of Him.

MY SONG OF PRAISE
by W. Monson

Oh, Jesus, Lord, I find no words that can express,
Your awesome love, Your sovereign purity.
By worldly wealth, You measure not success.
The treasures of Your kingdom come to even me.

When we allow Your Spirit to change our carnal hearts,
Only then will we, indeed, can we begin to know,
You, the Holy Son of God,
The Way, The Truth, The Life,
Your love and peace, Your joy as we began to grow.

Oh, Jesus, Lord, You suffer long,
Though often turned away.
Still at the Father's throne, You plead our cause.
Your Presence is our light each dark confusing day,
Refreshing us as at Your feet we humbly pause.

Though on our journey through this life we suffer too,
Before us goes the cross on which You paved the way.
Affording us, Your sinful saints, a guiltless avenue,
That cost Your life, and left no debt of sin for us to pay.

I do not know how long my journey in this life will be,
But I know Whom I believe
And trust to guide
My way.
My Savior, who
With but one word can calm the stormy sea.
My Shepherd,
Who has brought me back each time I've gone astray.

"Beyond Compare" is dedicated to Sambu and Carol Sissoko, Phoenix, Arizona, who are firm believers in God.

Psalm 48:10
10 According to Your name, O God,
　　So *is* Your praise to the ends of the earth;
　　Your right hand is full of righteousness.

Ecclesiastes 2:24
24 Nothing *is* better for a man *than* that he should eat and drink, and *that* his soul should enjoy good in his labor. This also, I saw, was from the hand of God.

BEYOND COMPARE
by W. Monson

Oh, God, Thy world is beautiful,
No matter what the season.
You trust it to the likes of man,
I know You have a reason.

Man usually takes all that he can,
Yet seldom thinks of giving,
Destroying beauty here and there,
And killing off what's living,

But let us rise above this stand
Reach out our hand and touch God's hand,
To recognize the beauty of
This world endowed with Godly love.

Oh, Lord, I pray that I may be
One who always is aware,
Lest self should blind, and I not see
Thy glory, far beyond compare.

"The Storm" is dedicated to people who are enduring difficulties and troubling times within their lives.

Psalm 55:16
¹⁶ As for me, I will call upon God,
    And the LORD shall save me.

Psalm 107:28-30
²⁸ Then they cry out to the LORD in their trouble,
    And He brings them out of their distresses.
²⁹ He calms the storm,
    So that its waves are still.
³⁰ Then they are glad because they are quiet;
    So He guides them to their desired haven.

The Storm
by W. Monson

The storm is great, my Lord, my God,
My mind is filled with stress,
As I cry out in deep despair,
"Help thou my helplessness."

Wandering through these darkened hours
Not knowing where to turn,
I once more for that quietness
And carefree spirit yearn.

Your sorrow, too, is great, I know.
Your heart feels all my pain.
Though dark clouds gather 'round about,
Your light still shines within.

Oh, lead me through this deep despair,
And vanquish all my fears.
Let my loneliness dissolve
In these penitential tears.

Then let me rise to laugh again,
My spirit mount on wings,
Till joy and praises flood my soul,
And peace Your Spirit brings.

"Eternal Rest" is dedicated to the memory of Zelma Mae Renfro, beloved of God and loved by her family.

Psalm 91:2
2 I will say of the Lord, "He is my refuge and my fortress;
    My God, in Him I will trust."

John 14:1-4
1 "Let not your heart be troubled; you believe in God, believe also in Me. 2 In My Father's house are many mansions;[a] if *it were* not *so*, I would have told you. I go to prepare a place for you.[b] 3 And if I go and prepare a place for you, I will come again and receive you to Myself; that where I am, *there* you may be also. 4 And where I go you know, and the way you know."

ETERNAL REST
by W. Monson

When dark clouds of this world
Tend to enfold me,
And it is so hard to see the light of day,
There is no other anchor that can hold me,
Except my Lord of whom the Bible told me.
As I this awesome recognition meet,
What need I, but lay my burdens at His feet.

Such turmoil in my mind, it overwhelms me.
Satan always tries so hard to make me stray.
But oh, what victory one day awaits me,
When Jesus puts an end
To him who hates me.
Then humbly at His feet, I bow me down,
And forever in His peace and joy abound.

By pouring out
His precious blood, God bought me.
For my sins,
With open wounds, the price He paid.
When like a sheep, I strayed,
He came and sought me,
And back into the fold
My Shepherd brought me.
He gently laid my head upon His breast,
Where I find the peace of His eternal rest.

"Oh Precious Name" is dedicated to Carol Hallowell, a witness for the Lord. Her website is for those who seek knowledge of the Gospel and for those who will become aware of the magnitude of God. Her website is at http://www.abbalovesus.com.

Philippians 3:13-14
[13] Brethren, I do not count myself to have apprehended; but one thing *I do,* forgetting those things which are behind and reaching forward to those things which are ahead, [14] I press toward the goal for the prize of the upward call of God in Christ Jesus.

OH PRECIOUS NAME
by W. Monson

Jesus...Jesus...Jesus.
The name I love to share.
I hear it in the gentle rain.
I know He's everywhere.

No other name so holy,
Nor to such joy gives birth.
Heralded by the angels,
And resounded down
To earth.

The lips of
Little children,
Oh, how they
Love to sing,
About the name of Jesus,
The precious Baby King!

His precious name,
So glorious,
So wonderful to hear.
It thrills my soul and spirit,
And drives away my fear.

I love the name of Jesus.
There is no other name,
Has wrought
So much contention,
Nor gathered
So much fame.

I have walked in
Deep despair,
Through clouds of
Darkest night.
His name has brought
The sunshine,
And bid the
Darkness flight.

When on the
Bed of sickness,
He always
Soothes my pain,
Brightening my tomorrow,
As I call
Upon His name.

Some day I'll bow
Before Him,
Free from my sin
And shame.
I'll kneel there and
Adore Him,
Whispering His name.

Jesus...Jesus...Jesus.

"I Thank Thee" is dedicated to Delores Renfro-Taylor, Goodyear, Arizona, a woman who loves, praises, and serves the Lord.

Psalm 113:1-3
[1] **Praise the LORD!**
    Praise, O servants of the LORD,
    Praise the name of the LORD!
[2] **Blessed be the name of the LORD**
    From this time forth and forevermore!
[3] **From the rising of the sun to its going down**
    The LORD's name *is* to be praised.

I THANK THEE
by W. Monson

I thank Thee, Holy Father,
For love and grace divine,
For the gift of glad forgiveness,
That through Jesus, You make mine.

I thank Thee, precious Jesus.
You left Your home above.
Came to be a lowly human,
Bringing me God's holy love.

I thank Thee, Holy Spirit,
My comforter so true,
For interceding with Your love,
As no one else could do.

I believe in God, the Father,
That Jesus sets me free
By the Holy Spirit's guiding,
Oh, Blessed Trinity.

"From Heaven" is dedicated to the remnant of Israel.

Malachi 4:5-6
5 Behold, I will send you Elijah the prophet
   Before the coming of the great and dreadful day of the LORD.
   6 And he will turn
   The hearts of the fathers to the children,
   And the hearts of the children to their fathers,
   Lest I come and strike the earth with a curse."

Revelation 12:7-9
7 And war broke out in heaven: Michael and his angels fought with the dragon; and the dragon and his angels fought, 8 but they did not prevail, nor was a place found for them[a] in heaven any longer. 9 So the great dragon was cast out, that serpent of old, called the Devil and Satan, who deceives the whole world; he was cast to the earth, and his angels were cast out with him.

FROM HEAVEN
by M. Monson

The army of the Lord was in the right.
Michael and his angels stood to fight.
They spun the ancient serpent's head around,
And threw Satan and his angels down,
From heaven on down to the earth below.
From heaven by a mighty blow!
    Oh, Michael! Oh, Michael!
    We know that Lucifer fell down here!
    Oh, Michael! Oh, Michael!
    The angel with the heavenly spear.

    (Refrain) Turn your hearts to your fathers, children,
        Listen to what they say.
        Turn your hearts to your children, fathers,
        Teach them how to pray.

The army of the Lord is drawing near.
The brave and loyal prophet has no fear.
He sweeps the earth with chariot forces,
Flung along on winged, racing horses,
From heaven on down to the earth they glide.
From heaven on a mighty slide.
    Elijah! Elijah!
    The rider at the chariot's helm.
    Elijah! Elijah!
    The prophet from the heavenly realm.
    (Repeat Refrain)

FROM HEAVEN (Continued...)

The army of the Lord has fought to win.
God's own Holy Son has conquered sin.
God's new blood covenant from Abraham's seed,
Was sacrificed for ungodly deeds,
From heaven on down to the earth He came,
From heaven to bear the blame.
    Israel! Israel!
    The Lord delivered everyone.
    Israel! Israel!
    God gave the world His only Son.
        (Repeat Refrain)

Truthful Gems

Exodus 19:18
18 Now Mount Sinai *was* completely in smoke, because the LORD descended upon it in fire. Its smoke ascended like the smoke of a furnace, and the whole mountain[a] quaked greatly.

2 Kings 2:11
11 Then it happened, as they continued on and talked, that suddenly a chariot of fire *appeared* with horses of fire, and separated the two of them; and Elijah went up by a whirlwind into heaven.

Proverbs 22:4
4 By humility *and* the fear of the LORD
  Are riches and honor and life.

Joel 2:11
11 The LORD gives voice before His army,
  For His camp is very great;
  For strong *is the One* who executes His word.
  For the day of the LORD *is* great and very terrible;
  Who can endure it?

"Peace Be Still" is dedicated to Mohammad and Sharket Sumari and family, Phoenix, Arizona, who have a strong spirit of love for God and for family.

Mark 4:37-41

37 And a great windstorm arose, and the waves beat into the boat, so that it was already filling. 38 But He was in the stern, asleep on a pillow. And they awoke Him and said to Him, "Teacher, do You not care that we are perishing?"
39 Then He arose and rebuked the wind, and said to the sea, "Peace, be still!" And the wind ceased and there was a great calm. 40 But He said to them, "Why are you so fearful? How *is it* that you have no faith?"[d] 41 And they feared exceedingly, and said to one another, "Who can this be, that even the wind and the sea obey Him!"

PEACE BE STILL
by W. Monson

Has my God forsaken me?
Oh, no! He never will.
Yet, sometimes when I pray,
He seems so very still.

Must I then the louder cry,
So that He should hear?
Or must I solemnly tremble,
In silence and in fear?

Must I search the mountains o'er?
The forests, in despair,
Or swim the mighty rivers,
To find my Savior there?

No. I'll turn to Holy Scriptures
There for me to find His will.
Then hear the Spirit whisper,
"My child, peace be still."

"He is Our God" is dedicated to a woman of faith and prayer, Barb Davis with Bethel's Rock Assembly of God Church, Minneapolis, Minnesota.

Ezekiel 10:3-5
³ Now the cherubim were standing on the south side of the temple[a] when the man went in, and the cloud filled the inner court. ⁴ Then the glory of the LORD went up from the cherub, *and paused* over the threshold of the temple; and the house was filled with the cloud, and the court was full of the brightness of the LORD's glory. ⁵ And the sound of the wings of the cherubim was heard *even* in the outer court, like the voice of Almighty God when He speaks.

HE IS OUR GOD
by W. Monson

He is my God; I praise His name.
I praise Him in the morning light.
He is my God, how great His fame.
I bow to Him each noon and night.
All praise to Him, oh, Holy Son.
All laud and honor, Three in One.
I praise His name.
How great His fame.
He is my God! He is my God!

The angels in the heavens sing,
The cherubim and seraphim.
Their praises laud the Holy King.
In reverence, they bow down to Him.
The sun, the moon, the stars obey.
Each sighing word they hear Him say.
They praise His name.
He is their God! He is their God!

Dear Christians, come with open hearts.
Lift up your eyes to God above.
He halts the sting of Satan's darts.
And wraps us in His arms of love.
He is our God; let's give Him praise.
In joyful song, glad anthems raise.
Let's praise His name! How great His fame!
He is our God! He is our God!

*This art was inspired by the beautiful photographs taken by Leedra at http://www.photographybyleedra.com/"

"Free in Christ" is dedicated to Deborah Rinkel, Fargo, North Dakota, who knows and speaks of the salvation of the Lord Jesus Christ.

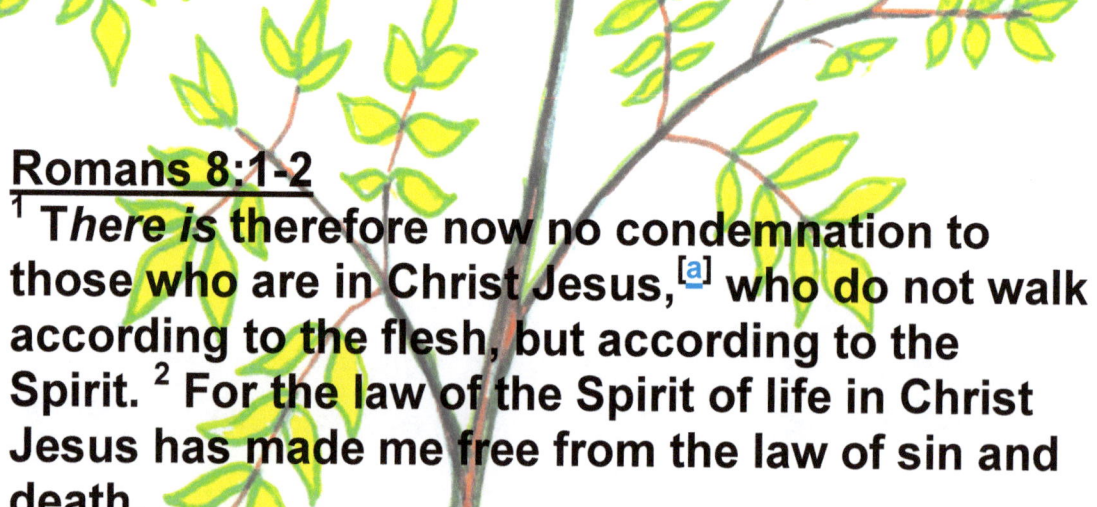

Romans 8:1-2

¹ There is therefore now no condemnation to those who are in Christ Jesus,[a] who do not walk according to the flesh, but according to the Spirit. ² For the law of the Spirit of life in Christ Jesus has made me free from the law of sin and death.

FREE IN CHRIST
by W. Monson

There's never a life without sorrow.
There's no heart that never has pain.
If we look to this world for salvation,
We seek it forever in vain.

We all sin and fall short of God's glory.
There's none righteous, that's why Jesus came,
To reconcile us unto the Father,
As repenting, we call on His name.

If we read God's word in the Bible,
He's given to show us the way,
We'll understand His plan for salvation,
And the price that Christ willingly paid.

So when to our life comes the sorrow,
Through the death of a dear one we've known,
'Tis the touch of God's sickle in harvest,
As He reaps in the fields He has sown.

We know that the Savior is waiting.
He's the way, the truth, and the life.
Welcoming us into His presence,
Free forever from sorrow and strife.

"Jesus is Everything to Me" is dedicated to Audrey Johnson, a woman devoted to spreading the gospel of Jesus Christ.

John 14:6
6 Jesus said to him, "I am the way, the truth, and the life. No one comes to the Father except through Me.

Philippians 2:9-11
9 Therefore God also has highly exalted Him and given Him the name which is above every name, 10 that at the name of Jesus every knee should bow, of those in heaven, and of those on earth, and of those under the earth, 11 and *that* every tongue should confess that Jesus Christ *is* Lord, to the glory of God the Father.

JESUS IS EVERYTHING TO ME
by W. Monson

Jesus is everything to me,
He is everything to me.
He makes my sorrowing heart to sing,
My songs in joyful praises ring.
My burdens to His cross I bring,
Because He is everything to me.

Jesus is everything to me.
He is everything to me.
From God in heaven to earth He came.
All sinners of this world to claim.
I glorify His holy name,
Because He is everything to me.

Jesus is everything to me.
He is everything to me.
As I have oft' His promises heard,
I stand upon His solid Word.
I trust Him, for He is my Lord,
Because He is everything to me.

Jesus is everything to me.
He is everything to me.
From God in heaven to earth He came.
All sinners like myself to claim.
I glorify His holy name,
Because He is everything to me.

"Jesus, My Joy" is dedicated to Joyce Tacker, the Director of Missions at the Glad Tiding Church, Casa Grande, Arizona.

1 Thessalonians 2:19-20
[19] For what *is* our hope, or joy, or crown of rejoicing? *Is it* not even you in the presence of our Lord Jesus Christ at His coming? [20] For you are our glory and joy.

JESUS, MY JOY
by W. Monson

I thank Him for the springtime's early dawning of the sky,
The tulips and the daffodils so pleasing to the eye.
Glad voices on the gentle breeze
As school days soon pass by.
For Jesus is the joy in my heart.
Jesus is the joy in my heart.

I thank Him for the summer days with chapel bells that ring.
I thank Him for the pretty birds that fly around and sing.
The butterflies that flit about,
The happiness they bring.
For Jesus is the joy in my heart.
Jesus is the joy in my heart.

I thank Him for the fall that changes leaves to brown and red.
The feeding deer that suddenly
Has risen up its head.
The waving fields of golden grain
That soon will turn to bread.
For Jesus is the joy in my heart.
Jesus is the joy in my heart.

I thank Him for the winter days when fields
Are white with snow,
And the morning frost upon the trees
That appear to glow.
With loving touch our precious God
Has made it all, I know.
For Jesus is the joy in my heart.
Jesus is the joy in my heart.

I thank Him for the bright sunny days of my life...and rain.
That He's always close beside me
Through sorrow and in pain.
Though dark clouds roll about me,
Soon His light will come again.
For Jesus is the joy in my heart.
Jesus is the joy in my heart.

"Oh, Dear Lord of Mercy" is dedicated to Clara Lee, Casa Grande, Arizona, who with faith and mercy, prays for others with the spirit of God in her heart.

Matthew 5:6-8
[6] **Blessed** *are* **those who hunger and thirst for righteousness, For they shall be filled.**
[7] **Blessed** *are* **the merciful, For they shall obtain mercy.**
[8] **Blessed** *are* **the pure in heart, For they shall see God.**

OH, DEAR LORD OF MERCY
by M. Monson

Oh, Dear Lord of mercy, I pray,
That You touch some little heart
Too small to walk or pray,
Who is crying, sighing, unable to speak,
A wet tear streaming down a cheek.
Send unto them the Comforter they seek.

>(Refrain)
>Oh, I am praying,
>Praying because of His mercy.
>He has made me trustworthy.
>I know His mercy is free.
>Oh, I am happy
>He has shown me mercy.
>He has called me trustworthy,
>Because of His mercy for me.

Oh, Dear Lord of mercy, I pray,
That You touch some lonely heart
Too ill to stand up tall,
Who is stooping without someone to call for,
Bending in pain, weakened, and poor.
Send unto them Your loving Counselor
(Repeat Refrain)

Oh, Dear Lord of mercy, I pray,
That You touch a saddened heart
Too dazed to see ahead,
Who is grieving, shaking, afraid in despair,
Thinking there is no one to care.
I pray for them Your most merciful prayer.
(Repeat Refrain)

"Christ in Me" is dedicated to Richard and Penny Stone, Casa Grande, Arizona. They give with their hearts.

Philippians 4:6-7
6 Be anxious for nothing, but in everything by prayer and supplication, with thanksgiving, let your requests be made known to God;
7 and the peace of God, which surpasses all understanding, will guard your hearts and minds through Christ Jesus.

CHRIST IN ME
by W. Monson

No matter what color is the sky,
For to me life still is bright.
I'm steadfast in the Spirit,
Who keeps me in the light.

With dark clouds all around me,
As I hear the thunder roll,
My trust is still in Jesus.
I know He holds my soul.

In my mind, there are times confusion
Seems to play the greater part,
But life cannot defeat me,
While Christ is in my heart.

God reaches downward in His mercy.
With His love, He floods my soul.
As I yield to Him my will,
Forgiveness makes me whole.

To confess Jesus is the Savior,
And admit we're not our own,
His Spirit will not leave us.
We need not walk alone.

He will enable us to reach out
To all who are in need,
As we live the Holy Gospel
In every word and deed.

"God Chose Me" is dedicated to all people who have come to the knowledge that they are chosen by God. They know that Jesus Christ was God's sacrifice for us. Jesus lived, died, and rose again. We can follow Him to eternity.

Ephesians 1:3-6
³ Blessed *be* the God and Father of our Lord Jesus Christ, who has blessed us with every spiritual blessing in the heavenly *places* in Christ, ⁴ just as He chose us in Him before the foundation of the world, that we should be holy and without blame before Him in love, ⁵ having predestined us to adoption as sons by Jesus Christ to Himself, according to the good pleasure of His will, ⁶ to the praise of the glory of His grace, by which He made us accepted in the Beloved.

GOD CHOSE ME
by W. Monson

I did not choose to know my Savior.
God, our Holy God, chose me.
He came and sought to save this sinner
Since far back in eternity.

    Before I was conceived, He knew me.
    Yet He loved me just the same.
    Reaching down in His grace abundant,
    When from my mother's womb I came.

        Though sin dwells in this chief of sinners,
        Yet He hears my every sigh.
        I'm awed to think in my condition,
        That He can love one such as I.

            He paid the price of my forgiveness,
            Bought me, sought me, found me, too.
            He is my rock when my strength fails me,
            He is my friend so kind and true.

                Oh, what great joy that lifts my spirit,
                As His peace now fills my soul.
                His awesome gift I cannot merit;
                He cleansed me and He made me whole.

                I'll seek to tell the precious story.
                Sing His praises day and night.
                One day I'll see His face in glory,
                There, shining forth in Holy light.

"Just Believe" is dedicated to Dave Byers, who has provided the Christian song writing organizations on the internet with free interaction for all singers and lyricists at http://christiansongwriting.org.

Psalm 119:162
¹⁶² I rejoice at Your word
    As one who finds great treasure.

Mark 9:23
²³ Jesus said to him, "If you can believe,[a] all things *are* possible to him who believes."

JUST BELIEVE
by M. Monson

You will save me from my enemies,
And throw my iniquities
Way down to the bottom of the sea.
You are righteous indignation,
And my retaliation
For all that the devil did to me.

(Refrain)
"Don't be afraid," Jesus said, "Just believe."
And I thank You, Dear Lord, for the faith I receive.
For I can have nothing, except what You give.
And You gave up Your life, so I could live.

You will heal my old afflictions,
And hurl all my addictions
Way down to the bottom of the sea.
You are loving reformation,
And lasting restoration
For all that the devil took from me.
(Repeat Refrain)

You will plan my fruitful ponderings,
And plunge my selfish wanderings
Way down to the bottom of the sea.
You are greater aspiration,
My very revelation
For all that the devil hid from me.
(Repeat Refrain)

"Stumbling Up" is dedicated to those who are struggling with sad problems in their lives.

John 10:28
28 And I give them eternal life, and they shall never perish; neither shall anyone snatch them out of My hand.

Hebrews 4:12
12 For the word of God *is* living and powerful, and sharper than any two-edged sword, piercing even to the division of soul and spirit, and of joints and marrow, and is a discerner of the thoughts and intents of the heart.

STUMBLING UP
by M. Monson

Oh, Dear God, You know my search
In this world is long and lonely.
It is low, low sadness that
Surrounds my lull in space.
And fainting stark and weary
From enduring wrong unduly,
I fantasize no bounds or ploys,
I'm stumbling up for grace.

There is nothing, Lord, I can do
But bear this fall and failing.
My broken heart attempts hope
For bolstering upright.
Oh, my God, with impending wrath,
Your sword will be impaling.
Pierce me now, spearing in your light,
And spurning on my fight.

On this dark battlefield,
If it is death I will be facing,
It is not a soul wrenched
Down to the grave in sorrow.
Only by believing
Eternal life is for embracing,
Will faith like this be showing,
In glowing joy tomorrow.

"Dear Lord, Save My Soul" is dedicated to those who are struggling with worldly and selfish temptations.

2 Thessalonians 2:16-17
16 Now may our Lord Jesus Christ Himself, and our God and Father, who has loved us and given *us* everlasting consolation and good hope by grace, 17 comfort your hearts and establish you in every good word and work.

DEAR LORD, SAVE MY SOUL
by M. Monson

Lord, wind a wedge of resistance
With resilient bathing brilliance.
Plant a hedge of protection
Of proportional perfection.
Display an array of angels,
An assembly for ascension,
From a ghastly laceration
And falsely promising sensation,
A life-draining, misleading, love-bleeding fabrication,
A birth quelling, pain drenching, hope quenching,
Pride swelling, earthly dwelling culmination,
A yawning, spanning jowl with a howling destination.
Lord, save my soul from Satan.
Amen.

■ "A Prayer for My Mother" is dedicated to mothers and sons and mothers and daughters who are separated by distance but are close in heart.

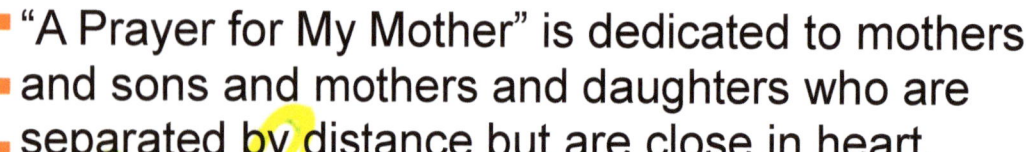

Psalm 126:3-4
³ Behold, children *are* a heritage from the LORD,
    The fruit of the womb *is* a reward.
⁴ Like arrows in the hand of a warrior,
    So *are* the children of one's youth.

A PRAYER FOR MY MOTHER
by W. Monson

Dearest Jesus,
Hear my prayer.
My dear mother's
Far away.
Keep her in Your
Tender care.
Hold her close to You,
I pray.

As years go by with speedy flight,
Make Your will her great desire.
Give her grace of peace and light.
Her joy in Thee a burning fire.

When at last Your whisper, "Come."
Her Alpha and Omega be.
Guide her to her heavenly home,
Perfectly at rest in Thee.

"God's Gift of Love" is dedicated to the memory of Bernice (Nowak) Dickey by her family and friends that knew her love and kindness towards others.

John 3:16-17
16 For God so loved the world that He gave His only begotten Son, that whoever believes in Him should not perish but have everlasting life. 17 For God did not send His Son into the world to condemn the world, but that the world through Him might be saved.

GOD'S GIFT OF LOVE
by W. Monson

How softly and how silently
The coming of the Lord.
He enters in the hearts
Of men by
God's own Holy Word.
Now hold Him close,
The precious one,
As Mary long ago,
Did hold Him close
And sing to Him
With shepherds bending low.
A tiny babe, a stable cold,
Yet warmth
Pours from above,
As born into humanity
Was God's own gift of love.

So softly and so silently,
Still moves the hand of God.
Our minds recall,
Our hearts lift up,
While bent from sorrow's rod.
Glorious light
Of heavenly joy, nothing
Else exceeds,
The grace that God
Has given forth
In fullness of our needs.
Oh, happy children,
All now come
To celebrate His birth.
No worldly wonder can outshine
God's gift of love to earth.

"To the Intellect" is dedicated to all who are blessed by God and seek faith.

Genesis 49:28
28 All these *are* the twelve tribes of Israel, and this *is* what their father spoke to them. And he blessed them; he blessed each one according to his own blessing.

Matthew 19:23-26
23 Then Jesus said to His disciples, "Assuredly, I say to you that it is hard for a rich man to enter the kingdom of heaven. **24** And again I say to you, it is easier for a camel to go through the eye of a needle than for a rich man to enter the kingdom of God."
25 When His disciples heard *it*, they were greatly astonished, saying, "Who then can be saved?"
26 But Jesus looked at *them* and said to them, "With men this is impossible, but with God all things are possible."

TO THE INTELLECT
by M. Monson

I ask you now emphatically,
With literal simplicity,
In researching faith philosophy,
I cannot see calamity,
Believing in eternity.
Can you?

Indeed, if it is reality,
That Jesus is our guarantee,
Never knowing death, we see
His face within infinity,
I want this very crucially.
Do you?

If you see some sensibility
Accepting immortality,
Then quietly and humbly,
I ask with hospitality,
If you would come to church with me?
Would you?

"What is Born Again" is dedicated to all people.

<u>John 3:7-8</u>
⁷ Do not marvel that I said to you, 'You must be born again.' ⁸ The wind blows where it wishes, and you hear the sound of it, but cannot tell where it comes from and where it goes. So is everyone who is born of the Spirit."

WHAT IS BORN AGAIN?
by W. and M. Monson

God said I must
Be born again.
What? Must I then
Crawl back within --
My mother's womb?
It's much too small
To hold me and
My sins and all.

What does this mean
To Christians now?
Be born again?
I wonder how?
I pray, Dear God,
That You will send,
One to define this,
"Born again."

God surely understood
My fear, as quickly sent
Was one to hear,
When from the church
That's standing near,
So promptly strolled
The minister.

A smile,
And then a handshake, too.
"Child," I'm asked,
"What's troubling you?"
"Please, Pastor,
Would you tell me when
I know that I am
Born again?"

A nod, and then came this reply,
"It's fear of death
From which you die.
Set free from guilt,
Set free from sin,
With faith,
You know you're born again.

"When you believe
God sent His Son,
The Savior, Lord,
The Promised One,
You know He died to set you free,
And saves you for eternity.

"The natural flesh
Cannot conceive,
The one in whom
You must believe.
The Holy Spirit in your soul
Will yield your will
To God's control.

"Baptized with water in the flesh,
The Spirit rises
From God's breath,
And breathes a new life into you,
Your mind, your heart,
Your soul is new."

"Yes, thank you, Pastor,
I can see
That Jesus gave His life for me.
He cleansed me from
My mortal sin,
And NOW I KNOW,
I'm born again."

Author's Note

M. Monson was born in a small town in North Dakota. She has been influenced by the Christian poetry written by her mother from the time she was a young woman. She read through the entire Bible when she was 8 years old. It was then when she first felt the presence of the Holy Spirit. She testifies about her spiritual experiences as follows:

"During a revival in our church, I stayed at the altar and prayed that I would receive a vision from God. A being appeared above me. He had a smile of love. His torso was gold, and His lower body was smoldering. Then, He reached down to His foot and pulled a ball of fire from it and hurled the fire down into my heart. Immediately, I thanked God for the vision I was given.

Among the numerous spiritual encounters in my life, one of the most glorious ones that I have seen was that of the heavens filled with many angels. Suddenly, appearing in the skies at another level, and in front of the angels and directly above and before me, was the Prophet Mohammed. He was praying to God up in the heavens. As he prayed, his eyes were turned upward and his features were obscured. He turned and prayed towards the East and then turned and prayed towards the West.

I did not hear his voice, but only saw him praying. Surely there is someone who knows the meaning of the prayers."

Is there someone who will stand in the gap?

www.ingramcontent.com/pod-product-compliance
Lightning Source LLC
Chambersburg PA
CBHW041544220426
43665CB00002B/34